FLORIDA SKETCHES
William Baldwin Follows Bartram's Tracks

≈

Letter Poems

Thomas Peter Bennett

Goose River Press
Waldoboro, Maine

Copyright © 2019 Thomas Peter Bennett

All rights reserved. No part of this book may be reproduced in any form without written permission from the publisher, except by a reviewer who may quote brief passages in a review to be printed in a newspaper or magazine.

Library of Congress Card Number: 2019951035

ISBN: 978-1-59713-205-3

First Printing, 2019

Cover: East Florida map by William Bartram, *Travels*, 1791

Published by
Goose River Press
3400 Friendship Road
Waldoboro ME 04572
e-mail: gooseriverpress@roadrunner.com
www.gooseriverpress.com

*"The attention of the traveller,
should be particularly turned, in the first place,
to the various works of nature..."*

—William Bartram, *Travels*, 1791

William Bartram's Travels, 1791.
Courtesy of the Academy of Natural Sciences, Ewell Sale Stewart Library.

FLORIDA EXPLORED IN BARTRAM'S TRACKS

Do you know Bartram's Travels?
Carlyle asked.
In classic coy correspondence
with Emerson, he wrote:
*Treats of Florida chiefly
has a wondrous kind
of floundering eloquence in it
and has grown
immeasurably old.*

Carlyle's next proclamation—
*All American libraries
ought to provide themselves
with that kind of book
and keep it as
a future biblical article —*
prompted others to seek
Bartram's ancient
and future testament
and follow
in Bartram's tracks,
as did
Baldwin in 1813–1817,
Say, Ord, Peale, and Maclure in 1817–1818,
Audubon in 1831 …
many others … and me.

ILLUSTRATIONS

William Bartram's *Travels*, 1791. *Courtesy of the Academy of Natural Sciences, Ewell Sale Stewart Library.* Alexander Wilson's copy. Author's photograph. p iv

William Bartram (1739–1823). Charles Willson Peale, 1808. *Courtesy of Independence National Historical Park.* p. 2

William Baldwin (1779–1819). Charles Willson Peale, ca. 1819. *Reliquiae Baldwinianae*, Frontispiece. p .5

William Darlington (1782–1863). John Neagle, ca. 1825. *Courtesy of West Chester University, West Chester, PA.* p. 5

Baldwin's Early Excursions into East Florida. *Map by Brad Sanders, 2019.* p. 9

Baldwin's More Extended Expedition into East Florida. *Map by Brad Sanders, 2019.* p. 22

CONTENTS

FRONTISPIECE

ILLUSTRATIONS

INTRODUCTION

PROLOGUE TO BALDWIN'S TRAVELS

    FLORIDA 1

    WILLIAM BARTRAM'S FLORIDA TRACKS 3

    REFLECTIONS ON WILLIAM BALDWIN 6

BALDWIN'S EARLY FLORIDA EXPLORATION

    EARLY ON 13

    AMELIA ISLAND 16

    A MEMORY 19

    ST. JOHN'S RIVER 20

A MORE EXTENDED EXPEDITION

    COASTAL EXPLORATION 25

    FLORIDA LANDSCAPE 28

    BALDWIN'S TRAVELS CONTINUE 30

ST. AUGUSTINE 33

SOUTH ON THE MATANZA 34

FISH'S ISLAND AND THE
      COQUINA ROCK QUARRIES 35

FISH 38

PEÑON ISLAND 40

HERNANDEZ PLANTATION 42

PLEASING HORRIBLE 44

TOMOKO RIVER 46

MRS. CARR'S 47

HALIFAX RIVER SOUTH 48

NEW SMYRNA 51

HOMEWARD BOUND 52

BACK TO ST. MARY'S 53

BARTRAM'S ERROR 55

HOME TO SAVANNAH 56

FLORIDA OBSERVATIONS

    SANDY PLAINS AND SWAMPY SOLITUDES 59

    THE LAND 60

    CLIMATE 61

    HURRICANE 62

    FLORIDA'S FUTURE 68

WILLIAM BARTRAM

    ALLIGATORS 71

    BALDWIN VISITS BARTRAM 72

    LANTANA BARTRAMII 74

    ANOTHER BARTRAM VISIT 75

FLORIDA LETTERS

    CAETERA DESUNT 79

    AFTERWARD 80

POSTSCRIPTS

    BALDWIN CHRONOLOGY 85

    BIBLIOGRAPHY 88

POEM REFERENCE 91

ACKNOWLEDGMENTS 94

ABOUT THE AUTHOR 95

INTRODUCTION

FLORIDA SKETCHES: William Baldwin Follows Bartram's Tracks is a collection of poetry based on letters written during Baldwin's travels (1813-1817) along William Bartram's Florida trails. William Bartram (1739-1823)—the revered botanist and early American explorer of Florida—and his *Travels* (1791) are introduced to the reader in the frontispiece with a poem and a photograph of his classic work. The poems in the prologue set the scene in Florida, describe Bartram's explorations and introduce William Baldwin (1779-1819) and William Darlington (1782-1863). These men were the two primary correspondents in this book's saga of Baldwin's journeys to verify the botanical discoveries in Bartram's *Travels*. Darlington encouraged Baldwin to collect his Florida botanical letters into a publication. Alas, the death of Baldwin left the project unfinished.

Baldwin and his botanical exploration of Florida have been discussed in scholarly articles and books on botany and its history. Baldwin—like many explorers who visited Florida—was following in the footsteps of Bartram's *Travels*, intent on extending Bartram's studies of Florida's exotic flora.

Baldwin's travels and botanical studies in Florida are best known through his plant collections and specimens now curated in many natural history museums, as well as his letters to fellow botanists. While he published few botany articles, his letters, manuscripts, and specimens continue to be mined for information. During Baldwin's time, a number of scientists questioned the veracity of some of the observations Bartram recorded in *Travels*. Many botanists urged Baldwin, who was living in Georgia and exploring Florida, to confirm Bartram's observations, if possible. The narrative of this poetry collection focuses on Baldwin's journey along Bartram's tracks in Spanish East Florida.

After Baldwin's death in 1819 during a western expedition led by Stephen Long, Darlington—Baldwin's medical school friend and fellow botanist—collected, selected, and published many of his letters as *Reliquiae Baldwinianae*. Baldwin's letters recounting his Florida explorations and those related to Bartram were the sparks and sources for the poems in this book.

Most of the letters chosen for poems in this work come from Baldwin's correspondence with Darlington, then serving as a United States representative in Washington, D.C. The letters and other resources used in this poetry collection are detailed in the bibliography and poem references. Many poems are entirely original. Those poems that use letters as sources rely on Baldwin's or Darlington's language and the writing style of the 1800s. In a sense, I am both the author and editor of this work, which combines science, history, and poetry.

Those of Baldwin's letters selected as sources for poems are referenced. A stylistic choice was made to retain Baldwin's voice from 1812–1817 in the poetry narrative. Sequences and fragments of correspondence have been reordered, quoted, and paraphrased with new line breaks. For this reason, neither quotation marks nor sic are used for borrowed and poetically translated text. Italics are used for scientific names, following Baldwin's usage. Baldwin's style has been retained, as have his spellings for location names. For example, Baldwin's St. John's is St. Johns today, Tomoko is Tomoka, and Matanza is Matanzas. Baldwin and his colleagues used a variety of names to refer to his proposed publication about his Florida observations, including: "Notices of East Florida," "Florida Letters," "Floridian Letters," "Sketches of East Florida," and "Florida Sketches."

My writing was inspired by the 2018 Southern Garden History Society Conference in Jacksonville, Florida, on the St. Johns River, and a week spent exploring St. Marys, Cumberland Island, and Amelia Island. I had recently been researching and writing about Baldwin for another project. Familiar with Bartram's earlier explorations in the area, I became enchanted by Baldwin's descriptions of his own travels. My hope is that, through poetry, I can bring to light Baldwin's esoteric and descriptive letters about Florida and increase their interest and standing among art and science readers and Bartram enthusiasts.

Thomas Peter Bennett, 2019

PROLOGUE TO BALDWIN'S TRAVELS

FLORIDA

Mysterious, exotic Florida ...
    from earliest reports
in geological and climatic time,
    mastodons, rhinos, saber cats,
12,000-year-old human relics,
    to the Native peoples' first encounters
in 1513 when the Spanish arrived.

Spain ruled La Florida until 1763,
    when Spanish Florida became
Great Britain's fourteenth and fifteenth colonies,
    East and West Florida.

In 1765, King George III
    appointed John Bartram
—Philadelphian, plantsman, and botanist—
    as royal botanist
for the British Floridas.

Bartram's mission was to explore,
    beginning with the East Florida colony,
and document the Floridas' natural resources.

William Bartram (1739–1823).
Portrait by Charles Willson Peale, 1808.
Courtesy of Independence National Historical Park.

WILLIAM BARTRAM'S FLORIDA TRACKS

In 1765–1766,
    John Bartram and his son William,
a talented artist and field assistant,
    explored upper, northeast Florida
and the St. John's River.

William returned in 1773
    to explore both East and West Florida.

Florida continued as two British colonies
    throughout the American Revolution,
and in accordance with the treaties ending the conflict,
    East and West Florida again became
Spanish holdings in 1783.
    Florida's Second Spanish Period began.

William Bartram returned
    to his father's garden
in Philadelphia in 1777
    and wrote his classic

TRAVELS,
THROUGH
NORTH AND SOUTH CAROLINA,
GEORGIA,
EAST AND WEST FLORIDA ...,

published in 1791 in Philadelphia.

Many readers were eager to confirm Bartram's
 exotic accounts of Florida's
plants, birds, snakes, alligators, and other creatures.
 Whether they were fact or fantasy
was often the question
 botanists and zoologists asked.

Some explorers became armchair travelers,
 readers seeking specimens and information
from those who trekked in Bartram's tracks,
 using *Travels* as their guidebook and map.

William Baldwin was among
 the first in a chain of explorers
who followed Bartram's *Travels*,
 during Florida's Second Spanish Period,
literally in Bartram's tracks.

Throughout Baldwin's Florida excursions
 from 1813 through 1817,
he sent many letters and specimens
 and observations to botanist friends—
Henry Muhlenberg, William Darlington, Stephen Elliott,
 and others—
 often with permission to publish his
discoveries and East Florida letters.

William Baldwin (1779–1819). Portrait by Charles Willson Peale, ca. 1819.
Reliquiae Baldwinianae, Frontispiece.

William Darlington (1782–1863). Portrait by John Neagle, ca. 1825.
Courtesy of West Chester University, West Chester, PA.

REFLECTIONS ON WILLIAM BALDWIN

WILLIAM DARLINGTON wrote
    of his friend WILLIAM BALDWIN:

I was his classmate in our first course
    in medical lectures,
at the University of Pennsylvania,
    in the winter of 1802–3,
and we first formed
    that acquaintance, friendship,
terminated only with his life in 1819.

Early in the course,
    it was my misfortune
to have a severe attack of disease,
    which confined me for some time
to my solitary chamber in a boarding-house.

My classmates,
    even those who personally knew me,
never took a thought of the cause
    of my absence from my seat.

But not so with my friend BALDWIN.
    His sympathy for affliction
was always ready for action.

He promptly sought me out,
    devoted to me every hour he could command —
night and day, during my illness,
    like a ministering angel,
hovering round my bed

                                     (continued)

      with all the solacing attentions
of the kindest nurse and physician.

Later, while pursuing medical practice,
      we often corresponded about
many topics but, most of all, about
      our continuing interest in botanical studies,
he having become a practicing botanist.

In January 1817, while he was
      serving as a U.S. Navy physician
on the border of Spanish Florida,
      I sent a friendship letter
from Washington City
      to renew our acquaintance and
to discuss botany and Florida.

His lengthy response was
      one of many
among his future letters
      that I remember well.

From St. Mary's, Georgia
      BALDWIN wrote to me:
Your interesting letter of the 9th ultimo
      met me yesterday morning at Fernandina
(Amelia Island) on my return from an excursion
      in the adjoining province of East Florida.

It gives me great pleasure to learn
      that you are becoming
a devoted lover of botany.

I continue to be fond of that science
    and shall be glad to communicate
any information relating to it
    within the compass of my power.

My excursions into East Florida
    will also enable me to confirm
some of our good old friend BARTRAM'S
    doubtful plants.

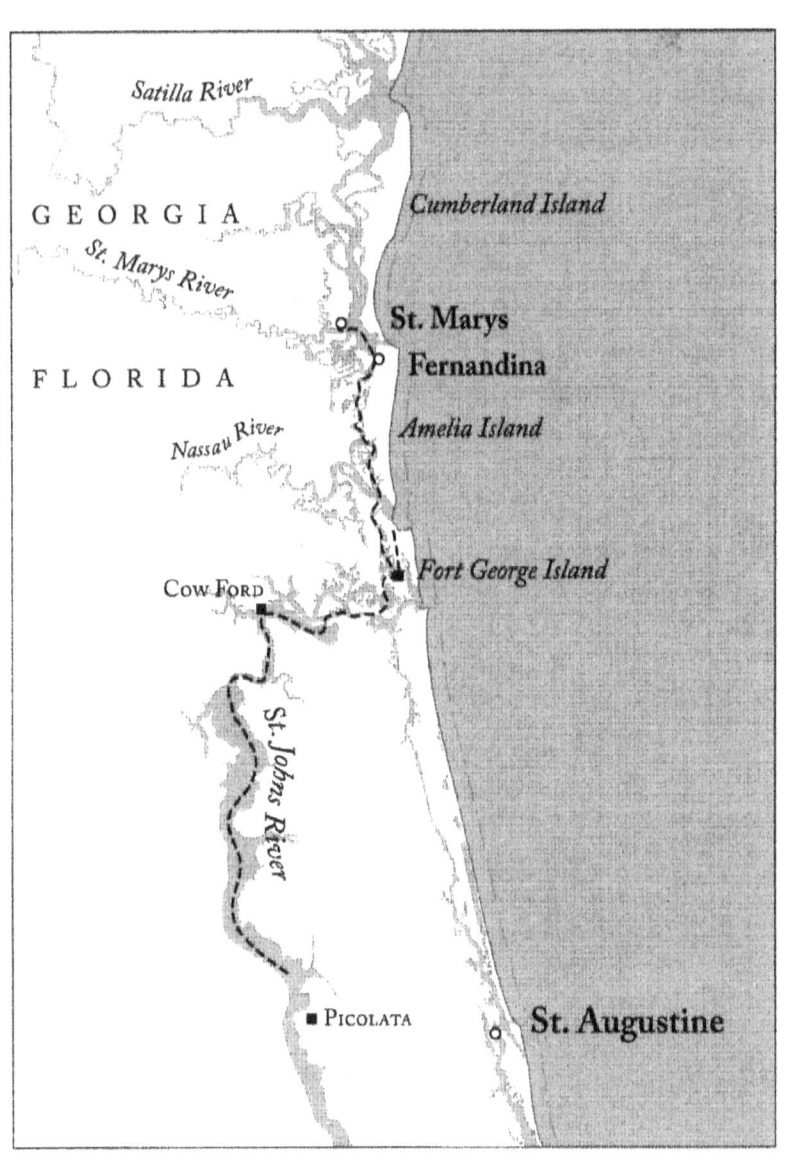

*Baldwin's Early Excursions into East Florida.
Map by Brad Sanders, 2019.*

BALDWIN'S EARLY FLORIDA EXPLORATION

EARLY ON
January 15, 1817

While returning to Savannah
    from Florida, Baldwin wrote
from St. Mary's, Georgia:

MY DEAR OLD FRIEND:
    Your interesting letter
met me at Fernandina (Amelia Island)
    on my return from an excursion
among the Dons
    in the adjoining province
of East Florida.

Several years' residence
    in this land of flowers,
where I have had
    opportunities for extended
excursions almost
    beyond the region of frost,
has enabled me
    to add a few new
and undescribed plants
    to our Southern catalogue,
some of which will be published
    in the work of Mr. ELLIOTT,
perhaps the whole
    in an appendix to that work,
should I find the leisure
    to complete my descriptions of them.

My present excursion into Florida
        will also enable me to confirm
some of our good old friend
        BARTRAM'S doubtful plants.

I have found his
        Lantana Camara,
Crinum, and a few others
        not noticed since
by any botanist.

I met the *Lantana*
        still flowering
on the Island of Fort George
        in December.

His *Crinum* is now not
        to be found on St. Simon's
but is abundant
        on Amelia Island
and in many
        places along the St. John's River.

I had a delightful excursion
        up the St. John's
—nearly as high as Picolata—
        and am now engaged in
packing up the roots and seeds,

        of which I have collected many,
to send to my botanical friends
        in Charleston and elsewhere
to be cultivated
        in order to complete their descriptions.

I have contemplated
    making a still more extensive
excursion to Florida
    during a more interesting season.

Not expecting when I left Savannah
    to travel much in Florida,
I carried no books with me,
    not even BARTRAM'S TRAVELS.
Next time, I will go better prepared.

AMELIA ISLAND
    December 8, 1816

The weather continuing warm
    and pleasant,
we had a delightful ramble
    for eleven miles
to the habitation
    of Capt. ROBERT HARRISON,
a wealthy cotton planter,
    who occupies one of the richest spots
on the island, within six miles
    of its southern extremity.

We took a middle path,
    through the most barren part
of the land,
    as the season
was not calculated
    to afford much novelty
in vegetable creations.

A little before we reached
    the aforementioned
plantation,
    we crossed near the head
of an extensive swamp,
    which, bearing northerly,
forms a small creek
    that empties into
the Amelia Sound,
    on the north side of Fernandina
(see BARTRAM, p. 65).

In this swamp is found
    an abundance
of the *Crinum Floridanum*
    of BARTRAM
—the leaves of which
    are still verdant.

I have only once
    seen
this plant in flower.
    It is a true *Crinum*
and comes pretty near
    the C. *Americanum* of AITON
but is probably a distinct species
    —noticed only by its discoverer.

I have long wished
    for an opportunity
to examine it
    more particularly
in the proper season.

Mr. BARTRAM
    first noticed it
on the Island of St. Simon's,
    near the town of Frederica.

It is still well known
    by the name of white lily,
by which it is distinguished
    from the *Canna flaccida*,
known by the name
    of yellow lily.

This swamp also abounds
    with the *Ilex Dahoon*.
Its clusters of red berries
    make a fine display.
This shrub attains
    a height of 20 or 30 feet
and may be considered to be
    one of the most ornamental
of this family of plants.

A MEMORY
    December 8, 1816

I cannot leave Amelia Island
    without expressing how much
I have been gratified
    by the unaffected hospitality
of its inhabitants
    wherever we have been
and by none more
    than the family
we are about to leave.

I became acquainted with the island
    in 1813
and shall ever remember
    what I experienced
on the night of the 16th
    and morning of the 17th
of September of year:

A Hurricane —
    of the force and character
of those that too frequently
    visit the West India islands
and other locations in
    and bordering upon the tropics —
which I will discuss later in "Florida Observations."

ST. JOHN'S RIVER
January 15, 1817

BALDWIN teases,
    entreating
his friend DARLINGTON:

Could you only
    come and go up
the beautiful St. John's
    along with me,
with what delight
    would we pursue
the steps of BARTRAM.

Baldwin beseeches his friend
    as he describes his
own earlier excursion.

Even now — I mean,
    in the middle of winter —
there are plenty of alligators
    to be seen and of an enormous size
in that river.
    And you may eat oranges
from morning till night
    at every plantation along the shores,
while the wild trees,
    bending with their golden fruit
over the water,
    present an enchanting appearance,
but the fruit is sour.

After traveling this river
        about 35 or 40 miles
in a westerly direction,
        it then takes a southerly course
parallel with the sea
        and may fairly be considered
to be a chain of lakes.

While at its mouth, it is not
        more than 1,000 yards;
at its first bend to the south,
        it is not less than nine miles wide.
You then pass on
        from point to point,
at distances of
        four and five miles,
the coves and points on each side
        corresponding with each other,
thus widening and narrowing
        until you reach Lake George,
which is twenty miles wide,
        the most extensive lake on this river.
Beside which,
        there are many fine lakes
at some distance from the river.

You pass out of the main river
        into narrow inlets,
which soon widen into spacious lakes,
        bounded by
rich and luxuriant shores.

But unless I could enter more largely
        and intelligibly into the details of these things,
I had better say nothing.

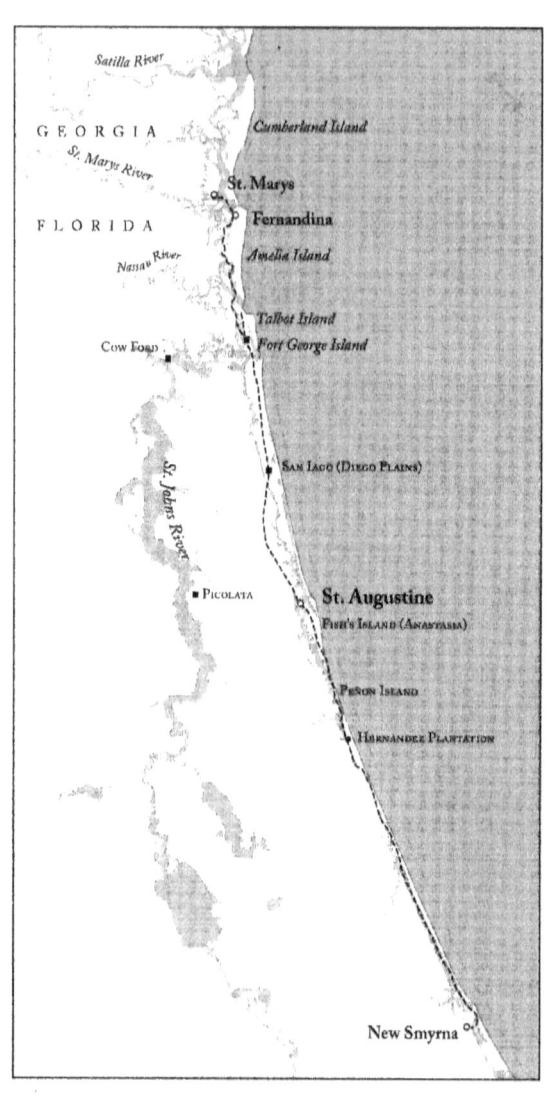

*Baldwin's More Extended Expedition into East Florida.
Map by Brad Sanders, 2019.*

A MORE EXTENDED EXPEDITION
—1817—

COASTAL EXPLORATION
March 30, 1817

From Prospect Hill,
    on Fort George Island,
Baldwin wrote to Darlington:

Seated alone on the summit
    of the highest land on the island,
elevated about 50 feet
    above the surrounding country,
commanding an extensive
    and varied prospect of the ocean,
the mouth of the St. John's
    and the various hammocks
and cultivated fields.

There is then,
    within a circumference
of about 20 yards,
    all to be recognized
from my seat:
    Magnolia grandiflora, Querercus virens,
Laurus Borbonia, Olea Americana and Ilex opaca.

But among all these,
    not one flower is to be seen,
and the only specimen of flowers
    that I have in my portfolio
after a ramble of two or three hours
    is *Hopea tinctorial (Symplocos, Wild).*

But think not that there are no flowers
    to be found on the island.
Although the season is
    at least a month behind,
there are *Cnicus horridulus,*
    a few specimens of which would fill a cart;
Scorzonera pinnatifida, Krigia Virginica, Houstonia;
    and the following, which may be new:
Galium, with very large hispid fruit.

One beautiful little *Lacerta bullaris,*
    the green lizard of Jamaica,
has made its appearance since I began to write.

Like the chameleon,
    this innocent little creature has
the faculty of changing color.

Could I only see a huge, "Magnanimous"
    (BARTRAM) rattlesnake,
it would help out
    my story very much.

During the five years I have been
    in this southern country,
I have seen but one living rattlesnake!

But had not BARTRAM been here before me,
    I would astonish you with my account
of the alligators.

I should like to wind up this
>   interesting botanical letter
with some notice of insects
>   could I call them by names less vulgar
than sand-flies, horse-flies, &c.,
>   which have been buzzing about
me since I began to write.

I must now rise and "advance backwards"
>   to Talbot Island.

FLORIDA LANDSCAPE
April 19, 1817

That kind of land
    that is here called *hammocks*
is generally
    covered with live oak.

It is a little elevated
    limestone,
still abounding
    all along the coast
with undecomposed
    oyster shells, &c.

But by far
    the greatest quantity
of land along the sea board
    is low pine barren
covered with *Pinus palustris*
    (long-leaf pine) principally.

Undergrowth,
    saw palmetto
with some fine shrubs,
    Andromedas, Bejaria, &c.

What we call *savannas*
    in this country
correspond pretty well
    with the *prairies* of the West.

But, *savannas* are seldom so extensive.
 The soil in them
is clayey,
 while the *pine barren* is sandy.

These are the most sterile
 of all descriptions of land.

BALDWIN'S TRAVELS CONTINUE

Adieu!
You may hear from me again
      from St. Augustine
should I halt there.

I have this day been examining
      one of the artificial curiosities
of the country:
      an Indian mound.

I find it filled with human bones
      deposited
in a particular order &c.

I am now travelling
      in a mode that exactly accords
with my objects of pursuit,
      viz, by water and by land
—on horseback, and on foot—
      in such a leisurely manner
as to afford me an opportunity
      of looking about as I pass along.

Dr. JONAS CUTTER,
      A worthy young Physician and
man of Science, accompanies me.
      We have one horse
to convey our baggage, and
      on which we alternately
take a ride to rest ourselves.

In this delightful manner,
    we have travelled
from St. John's.

We left Fort George
    before day on the morning
of the 1st, and including
    the distance by water,
we travelled at least 25 miles.

In the evening, we encamped
    at the cottage of an ancient
Minorcan on the borders
    of the plains of *San Iago*.

Here, we procured plenty of milk
    and feasted sumptuously
on a fat gopher,
    a species of testudo or tortoise
described by BARTRAM.

Our venerable old host,
    whose roof was thatched
with the palmettoes
    by which he was surrounded,
had not less than 200 head
    of fine, fat cattle,
with other stock in proportion,
    and he lived quietly
in peace and plenty.

He was one of those who,
> more than half a century ago,
were enticed from their native land
> by the famous Dr. TURNBULL
and experienced nine years of slavery
> at New Smyrna on the Musquitoe River
(see BARTRAM, &c.)

The plains of San Iago,
situated immediately on the sea coast,
about 15 miles south of St. John's,
> occupy a space of at least nine square miles.

The land is of an excellent quality,
> affording the finest range for cattle,
and this is all the use that is now made of it.

It would produce the finest
> sugarcane, cotton,
or almost anything which an
> industrious agriculturist might choose
to plant.

ST. AUGUSTINE
May 3, 1817

St. Augustine may be justly
        considered to be
one of the healthiest
        cities in the world.

Neither intermitting
        nor remitting fevers
are known here,
        nor have I heard
of a case
        of pulmonary consumption.

I exempt from this general account
        all sporadic cases of disease,
whether occurring among natives
        or strangers.

Neither, however, is it liable to
        those destructive fevers
that ravage most of the seaports
        of Georgia and S. Carolina ...

I do not know where to find
        a better country for valetudinarians.

SOUTH ON THE MATANZA

On the morning of the 6th,
    we decamped from St. Augustine
and, embarking in a snug canoe boat,
    travelled south along the Matanza River,
between FISH's Island and the Main.

At a few miles' distance
    on the western shore,
we passed an elevated spot
    that once contained
the habitation
    of Governor MOULTRIE.

A small cabin and a few date trees
    are all that appear to mark
the place where the hand
    of high cultivation
and improvement once extended.

At the southern extremity of FISH's Island
    and near the Matanza bar
stands a Spanish tower,
    where a corporal's guard
is stationed
    to look at folks as they pass by.

FISH'S ISLAND AND THE COQUINA ROCK QUARRIES
May 15, 1817

I am on
      Fish's Island ...
We have now made good
      our travel to 30 miles north
of Smyrna to good quarters
      for spending a rainy day.

The leading object was
      to see the quarries.

These are situated on a ridge
      that runs parallel with the sea
the whole length of the island,
      at a distance of one to two miles
from the beach.

The island is here about three miles wide,
      and the width of the testaceous ridge
is 300 to 400 yards, with an unknown depth.

The quarries have not been sunk
      more than 12 or 15 feet
as excellent freshwater obstructs
      all further progress downward.

But there is no necessity
      to run deep to obtain
an infinite abundance
      of this valuable stone
as it reaches in many places
      the surface of the ground.

Loose shells generally
        cover the surface,
below which is a thin plate of stone
        and so on, alternating,
the intervening loose shells
        gradually diminishing,
and the plates of stone increasing
        in thickness until they become
perfectly solid.

Stone splits with the utmost facility
        horizontally and is easily dressed
with a hatchet into the forms required.

A little to the west
        is a chain of sandhills,
which evidently proves
        that the shelly ridge was
the intervening beach where the ocean,
        in some former distant period,
rolled its waves along, depositing shells,
        now cemented together
by a natural chemical process.

I shall not stop to theorize,
        nor will I inform you at this time
of what kind of shells afford this stone
        as I do not know,
being but a poor conchologist.

I may add that the little animals
        that originally inhabited
these famous shells
        make excellent soup.

This island is twenty miles in length
        but contracts
near its southern extremity
        to a few hundred yards,
and here the shelly ridge passes
        across the Matanza River to the Main.

As you advance south, these stones
        become harder and, of course,
of a more delicate texture —
        but more difficult to manufacture.

They probably continue all the way
        to the cape,
certainly as far as
        the Indian River.

FISH

The evening proving squally,
    we were unable
to re-cross the Matanza River
    and took up our abode for the night
in an ancient and venerable fabric
    erected by old FISH,
the original proprietor of the island.

He was a native of Flatbush
    in the state of New York
and made land improvements,
    which have hardly
been exceeded
    in any part of the province.

Here are the remains
    of perhaps the most celebrated
orange grove in the world.

Some trees that remain
    are thirty feet in height,
and still retain
    a portion of their golden fruit.

But all is now in ruins.
    Two family generations
have passed away.

We were very politely entertained
    by two handsome young
grandchildren
    of the aforementioned FISH.

Their father was killed by lightning
> a few years ago,
and no one is left
> sufficiently qualified to keep
the premises in good order.

The quantity of good land
> on this island
is pretty considerable,
> and it is a delightful
summer retreat.

PEŃON ISLAND

Early in the evening, we encamped
        on Peńon (Rock Island),
situated on the northern shore of the Matanza Inlet.

This is a small, barren island,
        containing, however, a remarkable mound
of oyster shells, full of the bones
        of Aborigines, along with
the domestic implements
        with which they were interred:
earthen vessels, hatchets, &c.

We caught plenty of fish for supper,
        spread our blankets under the canopy
of a star-spangled sky,
        and, after a little persecution
from the mosquitoes,
        reposed in peace.

Our heads were defended
        by Spanish bayonets
(*Yucca aloifolia*).

The leaves of this elegant plant
        (which is now in flower)
are furnished at the extremity
        with most formidable spines,
and spreading out horizontally,
        they inflict serious wounds
when carelessly stumbled upon.

I have not been able to discover
    a *Y. gloriosa* distinct from this plant.

The next morning, crossing the inlet
    at the southern point
of Peñon Island,
    we traveled the upper Matanza River,
which, running south 10 or 12 miles
    close to the seashore,
originates from several heads
    in the swamps
a little westerly.

HERNANDEZ PLANTATION

One branch of the Matanza River led us
        to the Hernandez plantation
and coonti plants.

Tracing the eastern branch,
        we landed early in the afternoon
at the plantation of a Mr. HERNANDEZ.

Here, in a thin, sandy hammock
        of small live oaks, cabbage, and saw palmettoes,
I was gratified to find
        the wild sago, or coonti, of the Seminoles
and to assign it its place in the sexual system:
        Dioecia, Palganciria: natural order, *Palmae*.

I have no books with me to refer to,
        but it is probably a new genus
—approaching very closely in habit
        to the real sago family (*Gyms*).

At supper, I had the pleasure
        to eat bread
prepared from the large,
        tuberous root of this plant.

In the late times of difficulty,
        many Africans and others
were prevented from perishing through
        hunger by having recourse
to it, and the slaves on this plantation
        can save half their allowance
as a consequence of using it.

I have no hesitation in saying
    that it will be found among
the most important of our *esculeta*.

Bow-Legs, the grandson
    of BARTRAM'S Long Warrior,
says that "coonti" signifies "bread plant."
    This proved to be the *Zamia pumila*.

PLEASING HORRIBLE

We spent a whole day
        reconnoitering here,
and in a ramble near the beach,
        I had the pleasing, horrible prospect
of seeing a living rattlesnake,
        six feet in length.

He had the *generosity*,
        when unperceived by us,
to give the dread alarm.

But a sudden leap, I apprehend,
        alone saved my companion
from feeling the full force
        of his magnanimity.

Never have I seen anything
        so awfully, so horribly terrific
as this rattlesnake in anger.

Even the gigantic alligator,
        with his iron sides and formidable
tusks ever grinning horribly,
        with ghastly smiles, bears
in my estimation no comparison.

The fangs of this reptile were double
        and an inch and a half in length.

Nothing but the difficulty of procuring
      proper accommodations
for conveying him to Georgia
      prevented me   from saving his life
and taking him on with me
      to introduce to you
when I return north.

TOMOKO RIVER

From Hernandez plantation,
    we again took our land supplies
on board and reached this place
    (the Tomoko River)
on the evening of the third day,
    50 miles southerly of St. Augustine.

The land, I find, increases in fertility
    as we advance south,
the hammocks richer and more extensive,
    and even the pine land of a better quality.

From this place, we again took to the water,
    cruising down the Tomoko River
amidst shoals of alligators
    for three or four miles in a northeasterly direction
until we entered the Halifax River
    (a lagoon or an arm of the sea),
when we again bore down south,
    straight as a line could be drawn,
14 miles to the habitation
    of Mrs. CARR, a widow,
on the western shore.

MRS. CARR'S

Here was a noble, spontaneous grove
    of orange trees principally
the bittersweet (Seville) variety
    loaded with fruit of high perfection
and at the same time in flower.

Here, also, I discovered a species
    of *Myrtus* and a white *Blackberry*!

Recollect, I am only telling you
    part of the story.
I have seen many other new plants
    and fine things, too tedious to mention.

HALIFAX RIVER SOUTH

The night was spent with the widow,
        and the following evening,
we landed safely at the ruins of New Smyrna,
        about 16 miles further south
and the same distance from any settlement.

A short distance south of Mrs. CARR'S,
        we floated over acres of *Ruppia maritima*
—beaked tassel weed, widgeon grass—
        attached to a soft bottom of mud
and either floating or withdrawing under water
        as best comported with its pleasure.

Like the eelgrass *Vallisneria,*
        the stalk supporting
the flowers is spiral,
        some 10 inches
in length.
        The flowers are unequivocally
hermaphrodite and
        singularly constructed.

I amused myself for hours
        in attending to them.
Indeed, it requires some time
        and very close examination
to become acquainted with
        the fructification of this aquatic,
nor have I seen it accurately described.

I have no doubt

                                              (continued)

       it is the same plant
mentioned by all European botanists
       as a native of Europe.

A few miles further south,
       the river begins to wind
among numerous small islands,
       covered with the ever-verdant
Mangrove (Rhizophora Mangle, L.).

One of these small islands has
       been selected and occupied
for time immemorial
       by large grey pelicans.

Thousands were here assembled,
       feeding their young.

The nests, composed simply
       of marsh grass (*Spartina glabra*),
covered the mangrove trees
       as thick as apples.

We landed among them,
       and such screaming pelicans
could hardly be exceeded by Indians.

I was surprised to find among them
       great numbers
of the forked-tailed hawk.

These soon soared aloft and disappeared.
       Here and there also
was a hungry buzzard,
       watching to catch the offal.

Such a rendezvous of feathered gentry
    I have never seen,
unless it be the cormorants,
    which roost by the hundreds of thousands
on a sandspit running off the north end
    of Talbot Island.

But they were
    cormorants alone,
and not hawks, crows, buzzards,
    cranes, curlews, &c.

NEW SMYRNA

The fertility of the soil,
    the beauty of the situation,
and the extent of former improvements
    far exceeded my expectations.

The houses were all neatly built
    with those fine materials
peculiar to the country,
    but naked walls and chimneys
alone remained to mark
    the spot New Smyrna stood.

So luxuriant was the vegetation,
    that it was difficult getting along
without cutting our way.

Where the coach of TURNBULL
    once drove in triumph,
we found cabbage trees
    (*Chamaerops Palmetto*)
15 feet in height.

HOMEWARD BOUND

How I regret not being able to extend
    my research in this quarter!

It is time to begin to think
    of frying other fish.

I shall be the bearer
    of this letter
to St. Augustine,
    perhaps to St. Mary's,
intending now
    to make rapid marches.

BACK TO ST. MARY'S
May 27, 1817

MY DEAR SIR:
    I wrote to you twice from Fort George,
once from St. Augustine,
    and lastly from Tomoko.

Should all these communications
    be received, with this enormous one
immediately in the rear, they will
    altogether amount to something very
much like a bore,
    but that is nothing to me,
as I have fulfilled my engagement
    of writing "freely and frequently."

We returned from St. Augustine by a different route,
    traveling north by river 11 miles, and then
by land, traversed an extensive flat country
    immediately on the seaboard
and had an opportunity to see
    the whole extent of the Iago Plains.

We reached St. Mary's in the midst
    of deluges of rain
on the evening of the 25th.

It was with difficulty
    that I preserved
my collections from destruction.

I now find that my Coontia, or wild sago,
 is nothing more nor less than
BARTRAM'S *Zamia pumila*.

Could I have extended my excursion
 a little more westerly,
I should
 in all probability
have found many
 of BARTRAM'S
doubtful plants.

I am happy to say
 that his authority
is good in most instances
 where I have had
it in my power
 to travel over
the same ground.

BARTRAM'S ERROR

He is most defective in his
        geography,
and you rarely find his plants
        in the locations pointed out
in his TRAVELS.

One of the most extraordinary
        of his geographical blunders
is the mouth of the St. Mary's River,
        which he says enters the Atlantic
between Amelia and Talbot Islands.

How he could have made such a blunder
        is inconceivable,
and it has been copied by MORSE,
        and other geographers.

The St. Mary's discharges itself
        between Cumberland and Amelia,
twenty miles north of Talbot.

The waters of the Nassau River discharge
        between the southern extremity of Amelia
and the northern extremity of the Talbot Islands.

HOME TO SAVANNAH
May 28, 1817

On board the
    sloop *Hermit*,
Baldwin wrote:

I sailed from St. Mary's this morning,
    and we are now moving slowly along
through the Cumberland Sound.

FLORIDA OBSERVATIONS

SANDY PLAINS and SWAMPY SOLITUDES
Fernandina, December 6, 1816

Although the mere man
    of business or of pleasure
may see little to interest or amuse
    in the sandy plains
and the swampy solitudes
    of Georgia and Florida,
with the lover of botany,
    the case is far different.

He reflects that all-bountiful nature
    has clothed even the most sterile wastes
with some of her choicest ornamental,
    as well as useful, productions.

Who can behold
    the singular and beautiful
Befaria, or fly-catcher,
    without being charmed
by its splendor and fragrance
    or astonished at the faculty
it possesses of decoying insects!

The corolla of this plant
    secretes a tenacious substance,
which effectually retains flies
    and all other insects that alight upon it
until they perish:
    hence the name of fly-catcher.

THE LAND

There are no
        mountains
in E. Florida Province!
        Only a sand hill
about 50 feet above
        the surrounding land.

CLIMATE
May 3, 1817

A few loose observations
>   on the well-being of the climate
of E. Florida—

Above all, the salubrity
>   of the climate in this
province [East Florida]
>   must ever render it desirable.

But in the course of its cultivation
>   westward
and particularly on the St. John's River,
>   a sickly period must be expected.

I know of nothing that can occur
>   to interrupt the health
that is enjoyed all along
>   the sea coast.

Through the sultry months
>   of summer,
you are duly riled with
>   the trade wind,
and most of the tropical fruits,
>   with a little attention,
could doubtless be cultivated here
>   in the greatest abundance.

HURRICANE
September 24, 1813

I was sent for
        to visit a patient in great affliction
twenty miles distant,
        at the south end of Amelia Island.

I went prepared to collect all I could
        in this flowery department
but was disappointed
        by the state of the weather,
which, early the next morning
        after my arrival on the island,
exhibited tokens of a storm.

During the fore part of the day,
        the wind was variable,
with frequent showers of rain
        and some thunder.

In the afternoon,
        it gradually increased to a gale,
with the wind about northeast,
        accompanied with much rain.

I was in a house
        considered the strongest on the island,
inhabited by a Capt. H. with a large family,
        situated on the sound,
in sight of the Bay of St. John's.

At 10 p.m., the gale had increased so much
    that our safety became precarious —
as the house was cracking on its foundation —
    and most of the African dwellings,
corn, and cotton houses
    were already blown away.

In this situation,
    we abandoned the house
and retreated (men, women, and children)
    with great difficulty to a kitchen,
which, being low,
    was considered to be
the only place of safety.

Shortly after the house was evacuated,
    one of the chimneys fell,
and most of the windows
    and all of the outside doors
were blown away.

A little after midnight,
    the wind abated,
but it was only to excite
    more fearful apprehensions
of what was predicted to follow
    — and which, in a little time, took place.
The wind suddenly shifted to the S. W.
    and blew (if possible) with redoubled fury.

Such was the transcendent force of the wind,
    accompanied with torrents of rain,
that, in assisting to prop up the kitchen,
    which we had little expectation of saving.

                                        (continued)

I was blown off—
        or at least suffered myself to be carried
before the wind until I got hold
        of some piles of wood that had been driven
into the ground for a domestic purpose.

Here, it was with the utmost difficulty
        that I could maintain my hold
and prevent my face
        from being lacerated
with the sand and shells
        driven by the wind
in horrible confusion.

The rain, all the time,
        came down in such torrents
and was driven in such a manner
        as to resemble the waves of the sea.

It was impossible to retreat,
        and I remained in this situation
for about an hour,
        when the wind abating a little,
I (having been almost given up for lost)
        scrambled back to the kitchen,
which, though much wrecked,
        still remained on its foundation.

After 3 o'clock, the wind gradually waned.
        But what a dreary scene of desolation
did the light of day present!

Almost every neighboring house
        was torn down
or miserably wrecked.

Whole families had spent
        this dreadful night
unsheltered
        from the raging storm.

Not a flower was to be seen!
        Not an ornamental tree left standing!
The cotton and rice all destroyed!

In returning, I had to pass
        through a low, rich hammock,
consisting principally of live oak,
        but mixed with other oaks
and the great magnolia grandiflora.

Thousands of these
        were all prostrate,
blocking the way,
        and it was with
the greatest difficulty and hazard
        I could penetrate at all,
being frequently under the necessity
        of dismounting from my horse
to cut loose from grape vines, green briars, &c.

Nearly the whole forest
        was also under water
and in some places,
        up to the saddle,
so as almost to swim the horse.

Passing out of this
        into a pine barren
(consisting exclusively of *Pinus palustris*),
        every tree, of any importance, was prostrate!

I had next to learn
    that in Fernandina (the capital),
twenty-eight houses were blown down
    and every vessel in the harbor,
one brig excepted that had dragged
    on shore with five anchors.

It is, however, wonderful to relate
    that no lives were lost.
I had yet to learn
    the fate of St. Mary's,
—where all my hopes and fears were centered.

Here, on the morning of the 18th,
    I witnessed a similar scene of destruction,
and what was infinitely more melancholy,
    Gun vessel No. 164 had sunk,
and twenty of her crew perished,
    while the revenue cutter shared the same fate,
with the loss of two men.

The harbor was clear,
    while the city and adjacent shores
were filled with shipping.

I had the satisfaction,
    however, to find that
my little family was safe,
    having taken shelter
at a neighbor's house
    in my absence

But I am truly sorry
    to inform you

                                    (continued)

that my collection of specimens
        has suffered much,
and many of them
        are entirely destroyed
—among which
        are some of the rarest
from Creek country
        that cannot readily be replaced.

Had I been at home,
        with care,
they could have been saved.

The oldest inhabitants here
        observe
that this gale has not been paralleled
        in their memory,
even in this land of hurricanes.

But it appears
        not to have been extensive.
I learned that in St. Augustine,
        but little of it was felt
and that, in the opposite direction,
        its ravages did not extend
beyond Darien in Georgia,
        on the Altamaha.

Thus circumstanced, my dear sir—
        and also having many sick
and wounded to attend—
        I feel in a poor condition
to write anything
        that will be interesting to you at this time.

FLORIDA'S FUTURE
January 15, 1817

To WM. DARLINGTON, Esq.
    Representative in Congress, Washington City.
MY DEAR OLD FRIEND:

Do pray inform me
    in a confidential way
of what the determination
    of our government may be
respecting the Floridas.

There is not a decent man
    in the province of E. Florida
who does not wish that
    it belonged to the U. States,
as the Spanish government can afford
    no protection from the ravages
either of Indians or
    another description of people
called patriots.
    Let me hear from you immediately.

WILLIAM BARTRAM

ALLIGATORS
Darien, May 30, 1817

I paid a visit this evening
    to Mrs. SPALDING,
widow of — J. SPALDING, Esq.

This venerable old lady requested me to
    present her best respects
to W. BARTRAM,
    whom she well remembers
when, in days of yore,
    he travelled in Florida.
She says that his account
    of the alligators is not exaggerated.

BALDWIN VISITS BARTRAM
August 1817

Most importantly, BALDWIN was
    "anxious to see the venerable BARTRAM,"
and he did:

When in Philadelphia,
    after getting through
my business in the city,
    I paid the venerable
William Bartram a short visit
    on my return homeward.

Though far advanced
    in the vale of years,
I found him
    in possession of good health,
and all the faculties
    of his mind were as brilliant
as in the morning of life.

Such, he [BARTRAM] informed me,
    was his partiality
for that delightful country
    [Florida]
that he often fancied himself
    transported thither
in his dreams at night.

My ability to confirm
        several of his doubtful plants
was extremely gratifying to him,
        and he wished most anxiously
that I would return
        and find others of them
before he descended
        to the grave.

Aware of the suspicions
        of his veracity
that some entertain,
        I truly had a feast
to observe how
        his time-worn countenance
brightened up
        at the vindication of his character,
which I informed him
        I was prepared to offer.

So pleased was he
        with the little details
I gave him of East Florida—
        and so interested was I
in the information
        that he was capable
of affording me—
        that we parted
with great reluctance
        and mutual wishes for a further
and more intimate acquaintance.

LANTANA BARTRAMII
August 1817

With this visit to Bartram,
    I am prepared
to make his *Lantana Camara*
    a new species, without hesitation.

I saw the true West Indian camara
    in perfection, and I find it unequivocally
distinct from the Florida plant,
    which I shall describe and send to him
under the name of the *Lantana Bartramii*.
    It is an elegant plant.

ANOTHER BARTRAM VISIT
August 14, 1818

MY DEAR SIR:
    I spent several hours yesterday
with our worthy old friend BARTRAM
    and have made an arrangement
with Col. ROBERT CARR,
    who has management of the garden,
to cultivate my S. American plants.

He has now the *Lantana Bartramii*
    (for the first time)
in flower in his garden.

How would it answer
    to have an engraving
of this elegant plant
    as a frontispiece for my work?

Mrs. CARR
    (daughter of the late John Bartram)
draws elegantly
    and has engaged
to execute as many
    drawings for me as I want.

FLORIDA LETTERS

CAETERA DESUNT

MY DEAR DARLINGTON:
    Your observations on the plan
of my "Floridian Letters"
    meet my approbation exactly,
but I am not quite certain
    that the few
I have already prepared
    will agree precisely with it.

When you see them,
    you can judge,
and judge I hope you will
    with the most perfect
and unrestrained freedom.

In a later letter,
    Baldwin wrote:
Yours dated yesterday
    was handed to me
by your brother last evening.

I have not been idle
    since my return
from New York,
    but the state of my health
has kept me pretty much
    from my desk
and from close
    application to anything.

I begin to feel better
    and shall not
abandon the "Floridian Letters."

AFTERWARD
February 13, 1841

Darlington wrote to Asa Gray:

The notices of Dr. B.'s movements
    and observations in Florida
contained in his later correspondence
    were so interesting to me
that I suggested to him
    the project of his drawing up
a more complete account of East Florida
    in the form of familiar letters,
with a view to publication.

After some hesitation,
    he acceded to the proposition,
and had made some progress in the work
    as his health and engagements permitted
until it was finally interrupted
    by the reception of orders to prepare
for the western expedition under Major Long.
    His sketch was, of course,
left in an unfinished state.

Having recently had access to the original,
    I have ventured to transcribe and annex
a portion of it to the other epistolary remains
    in *Reliquiae Baldwinianae*.

This may serve to explain
    the repeated allusions
in his correspondence
    to the "Floridian Letters."

The recollection of his virtues
        continues to be fondly cherished
by every surviving friend,
        and his ardor in the pursuit
of his favorite science
        will render his memory forever dear
to true lovers of American botany.

POSTSCRIPTS

BALDWIN CHRONOLOGY

BIBLIOGRAPHY

POEM REFERENCES

ACKNOWLEDGMENTS

ABOUT THE AUTHOR

BALDWIN CHRONOLOGY

1779
William Baldwin is born in Chester County, Pennsylvania; botany is his youthful pursuit.

1802–1803
Meets William Darlington while studying medicine at the University of Pennsylvania. Studies botany with Professor Benjamin Barton and visits Bartram's and other gardens.

1807–1808
Awarded an MD degree by the University of Pennsylvania. Moves to Wilmington, Delaware, to practice medicine. Marries Hannah Webster. Continues his botany pursuits.

1811
Meets and begins a correspondence with botanist Rev. Henry Ernst Muhlenberg of Lancaster, Pennsylvania. Seeks relief from ill health due to pulmonary consumption by traveling to South Carolina and Georgia, a common remedy at the time. Botanizes and meets Southern botanists.

1812
Collaborates with botanists Stephen Elliott and John and Louis Le Conte. **June**—The War of 1812 begins. Becomes a surgeon's mate in the United States Navy and is stationed at St. Mary's, Georgia. **July**—Becomes a surgeon in the United States Navy. **October**—Returns to Wilmington and prepares to move his family to St. Mary's.

1813

February — Returns to St. Mary's with his family. **August** — Begins botanizing on the Spanish East Florida side of the St. Mary's River. **September** — Lives through a hurricane while seeing a patient on Amelia Island.

1814

Navy transfers him to Savannah and relocates his family. Frequently meets with the Le Contes of Woodmanston.

1815

The War of 1812 ends. Serves at sea in the tropics. His correspondent Muhlenberg dies. Returns to Savannah.

1816

Makes a botanical excursion into Spanish East Florida. Visits Fort George Island and Fernandina on Amelia Island. Travels about eighty miles up the St. John's River, arriving near Fort Picolata.

1817

January — Returns to Fernandina Beach on Amelia Island and travels to St. Mary's, where he receives a letter from William Darlington, a medical school classmate and now a United States representative from Pennsylvania who writes to renew their acquaintance. Replies and returns to Savannah. **March** — Leaves on a more extended excursion into East Florida: travels from St. Mary's to Fort George Island, Talbot Island, and fifteen miles south to San Iago ; returns to Fort George; travels to St. Augustine, Fish's Island, the Matanza River, Peñon Island, the Hernandez Plantation, the Tomoko River, the Halifax River, and New Smyrna Beach; and returns to St. Mary's. **June** — Returns to Wilmington and awaits naval deployment to South America. Elected a member of the Academy of Natural Sciences of Philadelphia. Visits William Bartram in Philadelphia. **November**—Sails for Rio de Janeiro.

1818

July—Returns to Wilmington. **August**—Visits Darlington in West Chester, Pennsylvania, then William Bartram and Col. Robert Carr and Mrs. Carr at Bartram's Garden. They take interest in his South American plants and proposed Florida publication. **September**—Darlington and John Le Conte recommend Baldwin for Stephen Long's western expedition to the upper Missouri River.

1819

January—Appointed to Stephen Long's expedition as a botanist and physician. Fellow botanist and Philadelphia Academy member Zaccheus Collins writes to Baldwin that the "Sketches of East Florida" is announced as forthcoming in *The Port Folio*. Member Joseph Correa de Serra suggests that the Academy publish it in its *Transactions*. **March**—Leaves for Pittsburgh and the west. **July**—Resigns from the expedition, suffering from chronic pulmonary consumption. **September**—Dies in Franklin, Missouri, and is buried by the Missouri River.

1843

Darlington publishes *Reliquiae Baldwinianae*, a selection of Baldwin's letters. Included are copies of eight letters Baldwin had chosen for his "Notices of East Florida."

BIBLIOGRAPHY

William Baldwin's letters are primarily drawn from a facsimile of the 1843 edition of *Reliquiae Baldwinianae: Selections from the Correspondence of the Late William Baldwin, M.D. Surgeon in the U.S. Navy. Compiled by William Darlington, M.D. (Facsimile of the 1843 Edition) Introduction by Joseph Ewan, Tulane University (Four Indices — of Persons, Plant Names, etc., Appended) Hafner Publishing Company, New York and London, 1969.* Darlington was the author, compiler, and publisher of the original edition (Philadelphia: Kimber and Sharpless, 1843). Baldwin's letters, specimens, and herbaria were widely distributed after his death, and many are in the collections of Harvard University, the New York Botanical Garden, the American Philosophical Society, the Academy of Natural Sciences of Drexel University — formerly the Academy of Natural Sciences of Philadelphia — and those of other institutions, often archived in the collections of his correspondents.

Travels is the short title for William Bartram's *Travels through North and South Carolina, Georgia, East and West Florida, the Cherokee Country, the Extensive Territories of the Muscogulges or Creek Confederacy, and the Country of the Chactaws. Containing an Account of the Soil and Natural Productions of Those Regions; Together with Observations on the Manners of the Indians.* (Philadelphia: James and Johnson, 1791).

Bennett, Thomas Peter. *A Celebration of John and William Bartram: In Philadelphia and Florida.* Indianapolis, IN: AuthorHouse, 2005.

Bennett, Thomas Peter. *Florida Explored: The Philadelphia Connection in Bartram's Tracks*. Macon, GA: Mercer University Press, 2019.

Cruickshank, Helen G. *John and William Bartram's America*. New York: Devin-Adair, Publishers, 1957, 1990.

Dallmeyer, Dorinda G. *Bartram's Living Legacy*. Macon, GA: Mercer University Press, 2010.

Darlington, William. *Reliquiae Baldwinianae: Selections from the Correspondence of the Late William Baldwin, M.D. Surgeon in the U.S. Navy. With Occasional Notes, and a Short Biographical Memoir. Compiled by William Darlington, M.D.* Kimber and Sharpless, 1843. Facsimile of the 1843 Edition. New York: Hafner Publishing Co., 1968. In addition to this facsimile reprint by Hafner (with an introduction by Joseph Ewan), other reprints of Darlington's 1843 *Reliquiae Baldwinianae* are available in print and online. These include the hardback Scholar Select edition available from Amazon, as well as the paperback edition in the Classic Reprint Series, available at www.forgottenbooks.com. All reprints are reproductions of the original work in the public domain in the United States of America.

Ewan, Joseph. Introduction. *Reliquiae Baldwinianae*. New York: Hafner Publishing Co., 1968.

Ewan, Joseph (Ed.). *A Short History of Botany in the United States*. New York: Hafner Publishing Co., 1969.

Gannon, Michael. Florida: *A Short History*. Gainesville, FL: University Press of Florida, 2003.

Harper, Francis. *The Travels of William Bartram: Naturalist's Edition*. Athens, GA: University of Georgia Press, 1998; reprint of the

1958 Yale University Press edition.

Hallock, Thomas, and Nancy Hoffmann. *William Bartram: The Search for Nature's Design*. Athens, GA: University of Georgia Press, 2010.

Juras, Philip. *The Southern Frontier: Landscapes Inspired by Bartram's Travels*. University of Athens, GA: University of Georgia Press, 2015.

Peck, Robert McCracken (Ed.). *William Bartram's Travels, with Introduction and Notes*. Salt Lake City, UT: Peregrine Smith, 1980.

Peck, Robert McCracken. *Bartram Heritage Report*. The US Department of the Interior and the Bartram Trail Conference, 1978.

Sanders, Brad. *Guide to William Bartram's Travels: Following the Trail of America's First Great Naturalist*. Athens, GA: Fevertree Press, 2002.

Schuyler, Alfred E. and Elizabeth P. McLean. The Versatile Bartrams and Their Enduring Botanical Legacy. *America's Curious Botanist*. Edited by Nancy E. Hoffmann and John C. Van Horne. Philadelphia, PA: American Philosophical Society, 2004.

POEM REFERENCES

FLORIDA EXPLORED IN BARTRAM'S TRACKS. Bennett, Thomas Peter. *A Celebration of John and William Bartram: In Philadelphia and Florida.* AuthorHouse, 2005, p. 1.

FLORIDA. Gannon, Michael. *Florida: A Short History.* University Press of Florida, 2003.

WILLIAM BARTRAM'S FLORIDA TRACKS. Peck, Robert McCracken (Ed.). *William Bartram's Travels, with Introduction and Notes.* Peregrine Smith, Inc., 1980. Sanders, Brad. *Guide to William Bartram's Travels: Following the Trail of America's First Great Naturalist.* Fevertree Press, 2002.

REFLECTIONS ON WILLIAM BALDWIN. Darlington, William. *Reliquiae Baldwinianae: Selections from the Correspondence of the Late William Baldwin, M.D Surgeon in the U.S. Navy. With Occasional Notes, and a Short Biographical Memoir. Compiled by William Darlington, M.D.* Facsimile of the 1843 edition. Hafner Publishing Co., 1968. p. 7-14.

EARLY ON. *Reliquiae*, p. 195-198. Stephen Elliott wrote *A Sketch of the Botany of South-Carolina and Georgia.*

AMELIA ISLAND. *Reliquiae*, p. 345-346. Historic plantation on south end of Amelia Island.

A MEMORY. *Reliquiae*, p. 346.

ST JOHN'S RIVER. *Reliquiae*, p. 195-199.

COASTAL EXPLORATION. *Reliquiae*, p. 210-213.

FLORIDA LANDSCAPE. *Reliquiae*, p. 213-218.

BALDWIN'S TRAVELS CONTINUE. *Reliquiae*, p. 218-221. "Dr.

JONAS CUTTER, a worthy young Physician and man of Science, accompanies me." Dr. Andrew TURNBULL was the wealthy British colonial investor and founder of the New Smyrna colony of slaves and indentured persons.

ST. AUGUSTINE. *Reliquiae*, p. 219–220.
SOUTH ON THE MATANZA. *Reliquiae*, p. 224.
FISH'S ISLAND AND THE COQUINA ROCK QUARRIES. *Reliquiae*, p. 222–223.
FISH. *Reliquiae*, p. 224.
PEŃON ISLAND. *Reliquiae*, p. 224–225.
HERNANDEZ PLANTATION. *Reliquiae*, p. 225. General José Mariano Hernández was a politician, plantation owner, and soldier. Bartram's Long Warrior; see Frontispiece *Travels*.
PLEASING HORRIBLE. *Reliquiae*, p. 226.
TOMOKO RIVER. *Reliquiae*, p. 226.
MRS. CARR'S. *Reliquiae*, p. 227.
HALIFAX RIVER SOUTH. *Reliquiae*, p. 226–228.
NEW SMYRNA. *Reliquiae*, p. 228.
HOMEWARD BOUND. *Reliquiae*, p. 228.
BACK TO ST. MARY'S. *Reliquiae*, p. 229.
BARTRAM'S ERROR. *Reliquiae*, p. 230.
HOME TO SAVANNAH. Reliquiae, p. 230.
SANDY PLAINS and SWAMPY SOLITUDES. *Reliquiae*, p. 344.
THE LAND *Reliquiae*, p. 213.
CLIMATE. *Reliquiae*, p. 219.
HURRICANE. *Reliquiae*, p. 109–112. Historic Capt. Harrison plantation on south end of Amelia Island.
FLORIDA'S FUTURE. *Reliquiae*, p. 198–199.

ALLIGATORS. *Reliquiae*, p. 232. James Spalding was owner of trading stores visited by Bartram during his travels.
BALDWIN VISITS BARTRAM. *Reliquiae*, p. 234, 238.
LANTANA BARTRAMII. *Reliquiae*, p. 233–239.
ANOTHER VISIT. *Reliquiae*, p. 277–278.
CAETERA DESUNT. *Reliquiae*, p. 235, 237, 239, 346.
AFTERWARD. *Reliquiae*, p. 5. Asa Gray (1810–1888) is one of the most important American botanist of the 19th century.

ACKNOWLEDGMENTS

With many thanks, I acknowledge the work of Joseph Ewan, who revived Darlington's 1843 *Reliquiae Baldwinianae* with the 1968 reprint by the Hafner Publishing Company and contributed insights into Baldwin's botanical studies with his introduction to that edition. Brad Sanders developed the maps based on my notes and our previous cooperative efforts. Gudrun Dorothea Bennett assisted my recent Florida exploration through her photography, critical conversations, and continuing support.

ABOUT THE AUTHOR

Thomas Peter Bennett is a Florida native on perpetual sabbatical as an independent scholar and poet. A former professor and natural history museum executive, he has published scientific articles and books, as well as poems and collections on topics featured in *Florida Sketches: William Baldwin Follows Bartram's Tracks*. This book is largely drawn from his research and field explorations along the Bartram Trail in Florida.

A graduate of Florida State University (FSU), Bennett earned his PhD in biochemistry from the Rockefeller University and became an assistant professor at Harvard University. He later returned to FSU as a professor and the chair of biological sciences, afterwards serving as the special assistant to the president and acting executive vice president. His museum work began with his appointment as the president of the Academy of Natural Sciences of Philadelphia, now the Academy of Natural Sciences of Drexel University. After a decade at the Academy, he returned to Florida as a dean, professor, and the director of the Florida Museum of Natural History at the University of Florida. Ten years later he became the executive director of the South Florida Museum and retired as an emeritus executive director.

While teaching at FSU, Bennett started publishing poetry, attended workshops with Michael Bugeja and others, and studied with Mary Oliver at Bennington College. Bennett's recent poems — inspired by the natural wonders in Florida and Maine — have appeared in, *Red Owl, Chebacco, POETALK, The Café Review,*

Puckerbrush Review, Pegasus Review, and *Perspectives in Biology and Medicine,* among others, and in various anthologies, such as *Goose River Anthology, Cosmos Club Poets Through the Years,* and *Bay Area Poets Coalition.* He is the author of several poetry chapbooks and five poetry books, including Nature, *As One Sees It* (2003), *A Celebration of John and William Bartram: In Philadelphia and Florida* (2005), *Hike On* (2008), and *Encore Seasons* (2017).

In addition to his poetry and scientific works, Bennett has several historical scientific books to his credit: *The Legacy: South Florida Museum* (2010), *The Le Contes: Scientific Family of Woodmanston* (2014), and *Florida Explored: The Philadelphia Connection in Bartram's Tracks* (2019). He is a member of The Explorers Club and the Cosmos Club.

www.ingramcontent.com/pod-product-compliance
Lightning Source LLC
Chambersburg PA
CBHW030529080526
44586CB00011B/370